U2

RATTLE

AND HUM

PRIDE (IN THE NAME OF LOVE)

One man come in the name of love
One man come and go
One man come he to justify
One man to overthrow

In the name of love
What more in the name of love
In the name of love
What more in the name of love

One man caught on a barbed wire fence
One man he resist
One man wash up on an empty beach
One man betrayed with a kiss

What more in the name of love
In the name of love
What more in the name of love

Early morning April four
A shot rings out in the Memphis sky
Free at last
They took your life
They could not take your pride

In the name of love
What more in the name of love
In the name of love
What more in the name of love

In the name of love

PRIDE (IN THE NAME OF LOVE)

WORDS BY BONO

MUSIC BY U2

one man to ov - er - throw. _____ In the name _____
one man be - trayed with a kiss.

_____ of love _____ what more _____ in the name of love _

_____ in the name _____ of love _____ what more _

_____ in the name of love. _____

D.S. and Repeat Chorus to Fade

Mmm _____ mmm _____ mmm _

_____ Ear - ly morn-ing Ap - ril four _ a

shot rings out _ in the Mem - phis sky. _ Free at last _ they _

_ took his life _ they could not _ take his _ pride. _ In the name _

SILVER AND GOLD

In the shit house, a shotgun
Praying hands hold me down
If only the hunter was hunted
In this tin can town,
No stars in the black night
Looks like the sky fall down,
No sun in the daylight
Looks like it's chained
to the ground.
Broken back to the ceiling
Broken nose to the floor
I scream at the silence
That crawls under the door
(under the floor).

The warden says,
"The exit is sold,"
If you want a way out –
Silver and Gold.
Silver and Gold.

There's a rope around my neck
There's a trigger in your gun
Jesus say something!
I am someone!

I seen the coming and going
The captains and the kings
Their navy blue uniforms
Them bright and shiny things
Yes, captains and kings
in the slave ships hold
They came to collect
Silver and Gold
Silver and Gold

The temperature is rising
The fever white hot
Mister I ain't got nothing
But it's more than you've got.

These chains no longer bind me
Nor the shackles at my feet
Outside are the prisoners
Inside the free (set them free).

A prize fighter in a corner is told
Hit where it hurts –
For Silver and Gold
Silver and Gold.

You can stop the world from turning around
You just gotta pay a penny in the pound.

SILVER AND GOLD

WORDS BY BONO

MUSIC BY U2

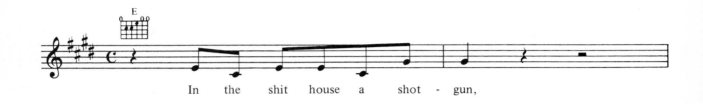

In the shit house a shot - gun,

pray-ing hands hold me down. If on-ly the hun - ter was hun -

ted in this tin can town, tin can town.

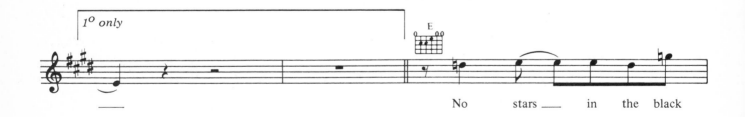

1° only

No stars in the black

night, looks like the sky fall down.

— No sun ___ in the day -

light, looks like it's chained to the ground,___ chained to the ground.

The war - den says "The ex - it's sold"___ if you

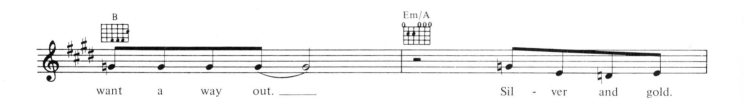

want a way out. ___ Sil - ver and gold.

To Coda ⊕

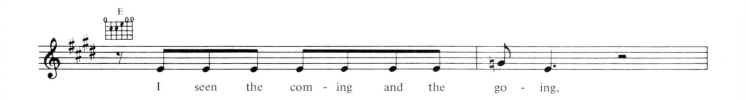

I seen the com - ing and the go - ing,

17

seen them cap - tains and kings, seen them na - vy blue

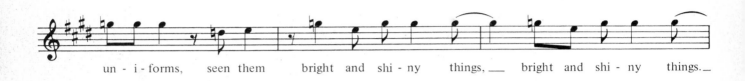

un - i - forms, seen them bright and shi - ny things, __ bright and shi - ny things. __

D.C. al Coda ⊕ *CODA*

INSTR. AD LIB.

VERSE 2:
Broken back to the ceiling
Broken nose to the floor
I scream at the silence
That crawls under the door

There's a rope around my neck
There's a trigger in your gun
Jesus say something!
I am someone!

Captains and kings, in the ship's hold,
They came to collect silver and gold.

VERSE 3:
The temperature is rising
The fever white hot
Mister I ain't got nothing
But it's more than you've got.

These chains no longer bind me
Nor the shackles at my feet
Outside are the prisoners
Inside the free (set them free).

A prize fighter in a corner is told
Hit where it hurts – For Silver and Gold
Silver and Gold.

HAWKMOON 269

Like a desert needs rain
Like a town needs a name
I need your love
Like a drifter needs a room
Hawkmoon
I need your love

Like a rhythm unbroken
Like drums in the night
Like sweet soul music
Like sunlight
I need your love

Like coming home
And you don't know
where you've been
Like black … as before
Like nicotine
I need your love

When the night has no end
And the day yet to begin
As the room spins around
I need your love

Like a Phoenix rising
Needs a holy tree
Like the sweet revenge
Of a bitter enemy
I need your love

Like the heat needs the sun
Like honey on her tongue
Like the muzzle of a gun
Like oxygen
I need your love

When the night has no end
And the day yet to begin
As the room spins around
I need your love

Like thunder needs rain
Like the preacher needs pain
Like tongues of flame
Like a blindman's cane
Like a needle in a vein
Like someone to blame
Like a thought unchained
Like a runaway train
I need your love

Like a fighter's rage
His dreams in a cage
Like faith needs a doubt
Like a freeway out
I need your love

Like powder needs a spark
Like lies need the dark
I need your love

HAWKMOON 269

WORDS BY BONO

MUSIC BY U2

Like a de-sert needs rain, — like a town needs a name, — I need your

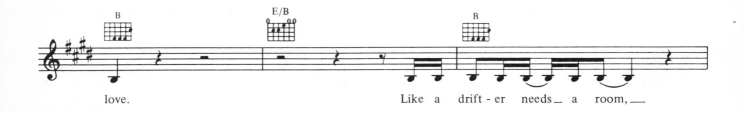

love.   Like a drift-er needs — a room, —

hawk-moon,   I need your   love.

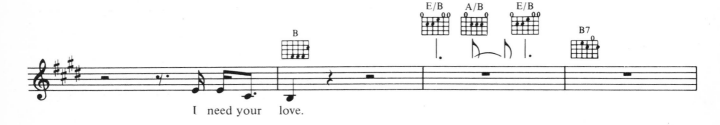

I need your   love.

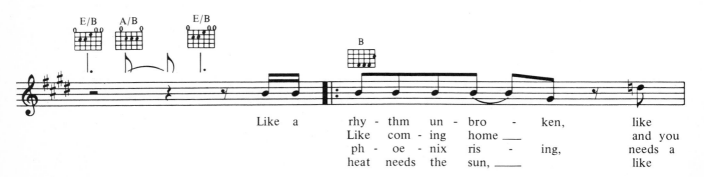

Like a   rhy-thm un-bro-ken,   like
Like com-ing home ___   and you
ph - oe - nix ris - ing,   needs a
heat needs the sun, ___   like

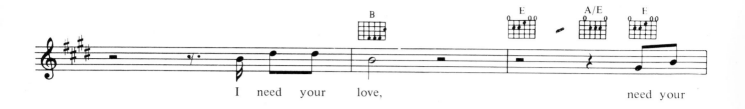

I need your love, need your

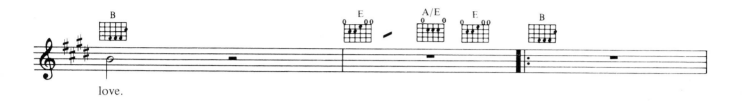

love.

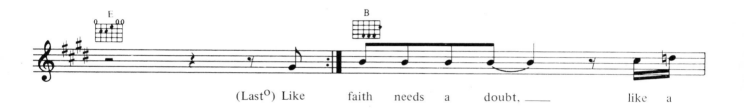

(Last°) Like faith needs a doubt, ___ like a

free way out, ___ I need your love. Like

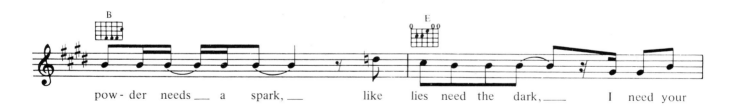

pow-der needs ___ a spark, ___ like lies need the dark, ___ I need your

Repeat ad lib.

To Fade

love.

HELTER SKELTER

When I get to the bottom
I go back to the top of the slide
Where I stop and turn
And I go for a ride
Till I get to the bottom
And I see you again

Do, don't you want me to love you?
I'm coming down fast, but I'm miles above you
Tell me, tell me, tell me, come on tell me the answer
Well, you may be a lover, but you ain't no dancer.

Helter skelter, helter skelter
Helter skelter

HELTER SKELTER

WORDS AND MUSIC BY
JOHN LENNON/PAUL McCARTNEY

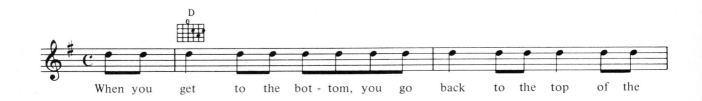

When you get to the bot - tom, you go back to the top of the

slide and you stop and you turn and you go for a ride, ___

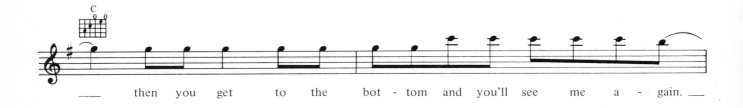

___ then you get to the bot - tom and you'll see me a - gain. ___

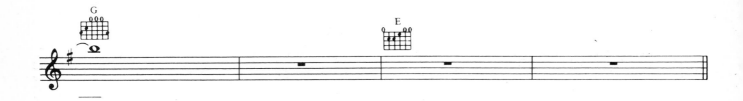

(1.3.) Do you, don't you want ___ me to love ___ you? ___
(2.) Do you, don't you want ___ me to make ___ you? ___

I'm com-ing down fast, I'm right ___ here a - bove ___ you. ___
I'm com-ing down fast, don't ___ let me break ___ you. ___

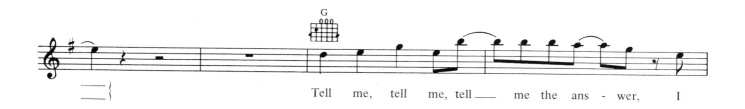

G

Tell me, tell me, tell ___ me the ans - wer, I

Am   E

ain't no lov-er but you ain't no dan-cer.

CHORUS

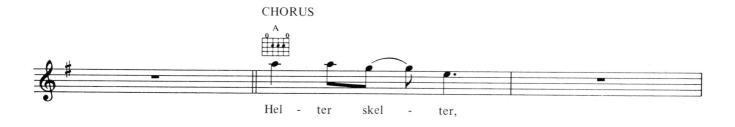

A

Hel - ter skel - ter,

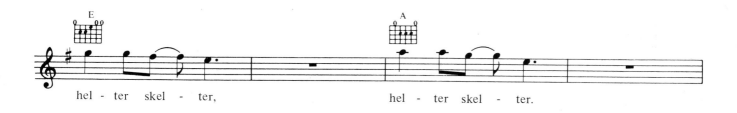

E   A

hel - ter skel - ter,   hel - ter skel - ter.

E

Repeat Chorus for Fine   *D.C.*

INSTR.

Ooh.

29

HEARTLAND

See the sunrise over her skin
Don't change it
See the sunrise on her skin
Dawn changes everything

And the delta sun burns bright and violent

Mississippi and the cotton wool heart
Sixty-six the highway speaks
Of deserts dry, of cool green valleys
Gold and silver veins – shining cities

In this heartland
In this heartland
In this heartland
Heaven knows this is a heartland

She feels like water in my hand
Freeway like a river cuts through this land
Into the side of love like a burning spear
And the poison rain brings a flood of fear
Through the ghostranch hills, Death Valley waters
In the towers of steel belief goes on and on

In this heartland
In this heartland
In this heartland
Heaven knows this is a heartland

HEARTLAND

WORDS BY BONO

MUSIC BY U2

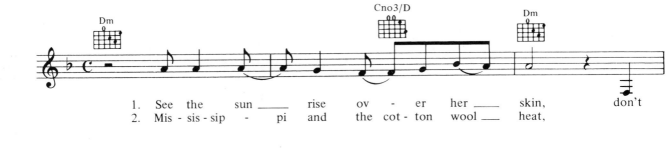

1. See the sun rise ov - er her skin, don't
2. Mis - sis - sip - pi and the cot - ton wool heat,

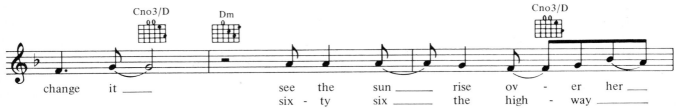

change it see the sun rise ov - er her
six - ty six the high - way

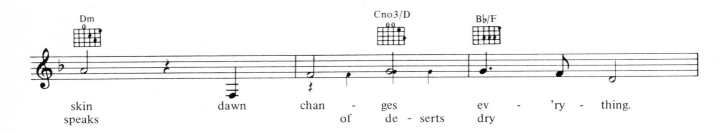

skin dawn chan - ges ev - 'ry - thing.
speaks of de - serts dry

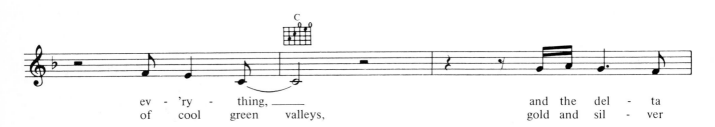

ev - 'ry - thing, and the del - ta
of cool green valleys, gold and sil - ver

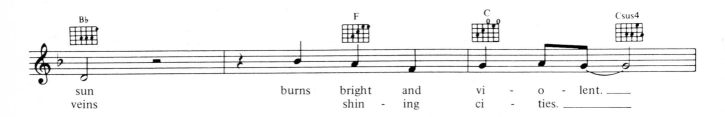

sun burns bright and vi - o - lent.
veins shin - ing ci - ties.

CHORUS

In this heart - land, _____ in this heart - land, _____ in this heart - land, _____ in this heart - land, _____

BRIDGE

hea - ven knows ___ this is a heart - land.

See the sun - rise ov - er her ___ skin,
she feels like wa - ter in ___ my _____ hand,
free way like a ri - ver cuts through this ___ land,

in - to the side of love
rain brings a flood of
hills death val - ley
steel be - lief goes

D.S. ad lib to Fade

spear, _____
fear, _____
wa - ters, ___
on _____ and

and the poi - son
through the ghost ranch
in the towers of
on. In this

DESIRE

Lover I'm off the streets
Gonna go where the bright lights
and the big city meet
With a red guitar, on fire
Desire

She's the candle
burning in my room
I'm like the needle
needle and spoon
Over the counter
with a shotgun
Pretty soon, everybody got one
And the fever when I'm beside her
Desire, Desire

(Burning, Burning)

She's the dollars
She's my protection
She's the promise
In the year of election
Sister, I can't let you go
I'm like a preacher
Stealing hearts at a travelling show
For love or money, money …?
Desire …

DESIRE

WORDS BY BONO

MUSIC BY U2

36

fe - ver   get - ting   high - er,   de - si - re,

de - si - re.   Burn - ing,

burn - ing. _____

She's   the   dol - lars,   she's my pro -

tec - tion,   yeah she's the pro - mise   in the year of e - lec -

- tions.   My sis - ter,   I can't let   you go, _____   I'm like a

preach - er steal - ing hearts ____ at a trav-el - ling show,   for love or

mo - ney mo - ney mo-ney mo-ney mo-ney mo-ney mo-ney   mo - ney mo-ney   mo-ney mo-ney and the

fe - ver   get - ting high - er,   de -

si - _____ re,   de -

Ad lib
to Fade

VAN DIEMEN'S LAND

Hold me now, hold me now
Till this hour has gone around
And I'm gone on the rising tide
For to face Van Diemen's land

It's a bitter pill I swallow here
To be rent from one so dear
We fought for justice and not for gain
But the magistrate sent me away

Now kings will rule and the poor will toil
And tear their hadnds as they tear the soil
But a day will come in the dawning age
When an honest man sees and honest wage

Hold me now, hold me now
Till this hour has gone around
And I'm gone on the rising tide
For to face Van Diemen's land

Still the gunman rules and the widows pay
A scarlet coat now a black beret
They thought that blood and sacrifice
Could out of death bring forth a life

VAN DIEMEN'S LAND

WORDS BY THE EDGE

MUSIC BY U2

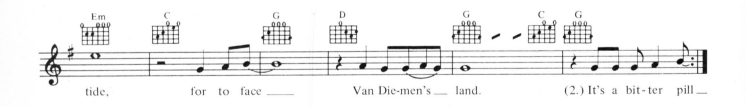

VERSE 2:
It's a bitter pill I swallow here
To be rent from one so dear
We fought for justice and not for gain
But the magistrate sent me away

VERSE 3:
Now kings will rule and the poor will toil
And tear their hands as they tear the soil
But a day will come in the dawning age
When an honest man sees an honest wage

VERSE 4:
Hold me now, hold me now
Till this hour has gone around
And I'm gone on the rising tide
For to face Van Diemen's land

VERSE 5:
Still the gunman rules and widows pay
A scarlet coat now a black beret
They thought that blood and sacrifice
Could out of death bring forth a life

FREEDOM FOR MY PEOPLE

WORDS AND MUSIC BY
STERLING MAGEE/BOBBY ROBINSON/MACIE MABINS

I need some free - dom, free - dom for my peo -

- ple. I want some free - dom.

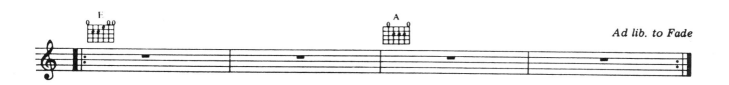

Ad lib. to Fade

FREEDOM FOR MY PEOPLE

I need some freedom
Freedom for my people
I want some freedom
Freedom
Freedom, freedom for my people
I'd like some freedom
I need some freedom for my people
Freedom
Freedom, freedom for my people

ALL I WANT IS YOU

You say you want a diamond on a ring of gold
You say you want your story to remain untold

All the promises we made from the
Cradle to the grave
When all I want is you

You say you'll give me a highway with on one on it
Treasure just to look upon it
All the riches in the night
You say you'll give me eyes on a moon of blindness
A river in a time of dryness
A harbour in the tempest

All the promises we make
From the cradle to the grave
When all I want is you

You say you want your love to work out right
To last with me through the night
You say you want a diamond on a ring of gold
Your story to remain untold
Your love not to grow cold

All the promises we break from the
Cradle to the grave
When all I want is you

All I want is you

ALL I WANT IS YOU

WORDS BY BONO

MUSIC BY U2

_____ is you. _____
_____ is you. _____
_____ is you. _____

To Coda ⊕

VERSES 2, 3

You _____ say   you'll give _____
You _____ say   you want _____

_____ me   a   high - way   with   no - one   on _____
your love to   work   out   right, _____

_____ it,   trea - sure   just   to   look   up   on _____ it,   all the
_____   to   last with   me   through the   night _____

2.   **D.%. al Coda**

rich - es   in the night. _____   You _____   _____   You _____

⊕ **CODA**

Ad lib. to Fade

‖ INSTRUMENTAL ‖

GOD PART II

Don't believe the devil I don't believe his book
But the truth is not the same without the lies he made up
I don't believe in excess succcess is to give
I don't believe in riches but you should see where I live
I ... I believe in love

Don't believe in forced entry I don't believe in rape
But everytime she passes by wild thoughts escape
I don't believe in deathrow, skidrow or the gangs
Don't believe in the Uzi it just went off in my hand
I ... I believe in love

Don't believe in cocaine I got a speedball in my head
I could cut and crack you open ... did you hear what I said?
don't believe them when they tell me there ain't no cure
The rich stay healthy the sick stay poor
I ... I believe in love

I don't believe in Goldman his type like a curse
Instant karma's gonna get him if I don't get him first
I don't believe that Rock 'N Roll can really change the world
As it spins in revolution spirals and turns
I ... I believe in love

I don't believe in the 60's in the golden age of pop
You glorify the past when the future dries up
I heart a singer on the radio late last night
Says he's gonna kick the darkness till it bleeds daylight*
I ... I believe in love

I feel like I'm falling, like I'm spinning on a wheel
It always stops beside a name a presence I can feel
I ... I believe in love

GOD PART II

WORDS BY BONO

MUSIC BY U2

Don't be-lieve the de-vil, I don't be-lieve his book, but the truth is not the same with-out the lies he made up. ___ I don't be-lieve ___ in ex - cess, suc-cess is to give, ___ I don't be-lieve ___ in rich - es, but you should see where I live. ___ I, I _____ be - lieve in love.

(6° Fine)

VERSE 2:
Don't believe in forced entry I don't believe in rape
But everytime she passes by wild thoughts escape
I don't believe in deathrow, skidrow or the gangs
Don't believe in the Uzi it just went off in my hand
I . . . I believe in love.

VERSE 3:
Don't believe in cocaine I got a speedball in my head
I could cut and crack you open . . . did you hear what I said?
Don't believe them when they tell me there ain't no cure
The rich stay healthy the sick stay poor
I . . . I believe in love.

VERSE 4:
I don't believe in Goldman his type like a curse
Instant karma's gonna get him if I don't get him first
I don't believe that Rock 'n Roll can really change the world
As it spins in revolution spirals and turns
I . . . I believe in love.

VERSE 5:
I don't believe in the 60's in the golden age of pop
You glorify the past when the future dries up
I heard a singer on the radio late last night
Says he's gonna kick the darkness till it bleeds daylight
I . . . I believe in love.

VERSE 6:
Love, love
Love, love, love
I feel like I'm falling, like I'm spinning on a wheel
It always stops beside a name a presence I can feel
I . . . I believe in love.

BULLET THE BLUE SKY

In the howling wind comes a stinging rain
See it driving nails into the souls on the tree of pain
From the firefly, a red orange glow
See the face of fear running scared in the valley below

Bullet the blue sky
Bullet the blue

In the locust wind comes a rattle and hum
Jacob wrestled the angel and the angel was overcome
Plant a demon seed, you raise a flower of fire
See them burning crosses, see the flames, higher and higher

Bullet the blue sky
Bullet the blue

Suit and tie comes up to me
His face red
Like a rose on a thorn bush
Like all the colours of a royal flush
And he's peeling off those dollar bills
(Slapping them down), one hundred, two hundred,
And I can see the fighter planes
And I can see the fighter planes
Across the mud huts where the children sleep
Through the alleys of a quiet city street
Up the staircase to the first floor
We turn the key and slowly unlock the door
A man breathes deep into saxaphone
Through the walls we hear the city groan
Outside is America
Outside is America.

BULLET THE BLUE SKY

WORDS BY BONO

MUSIC BY U2

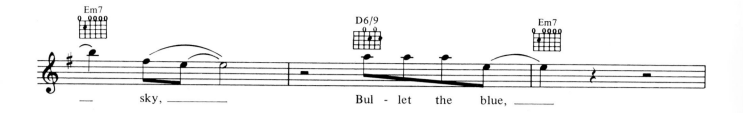

sky, _____ Bul - let the blue, _____

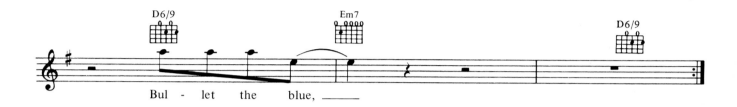

Bul - let the blue, _____

BRIDGE ‖*INSTRUMENTAL* ‖

* *(Spoken over rpt.)*

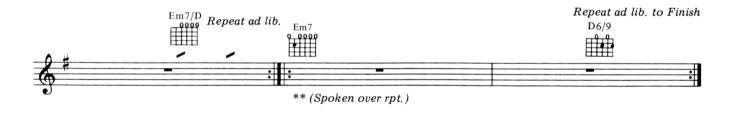

Repeat ad lib.

Repeat ad lib. to Finish

** *(Spoken over rpt.)*

VERSE 2:
In the locust wind comes a rattle and hum
Jacob wrestled the angel and the angel was overcome
You plant a demon seed, you raise a flower of fire
See them burning crosses, see the flames, higher and higher

* *SPOKEN:*
So this guy comes up to me
His face red
Like a rose on a thorn bush
Like all the colours of a royal flush
And he's peeling off those dollar bills
(Slapping them down), one hundred, two hundred,
And I can see those fighter planes
And I can see those fighter planes
Across the mud huts where the children sleep
Through the valleys and the quiet city streets
We take the staircase to the first floor
We turn the key and slowly unlock the door
A man breathes into a saxophone
Through the walls we hear the city groan
Outside is America
Outside is America.

** *SPOKEN:*
So back in the hotel room with John Coltrane
The Love Supreme
In the next room I hear some woman scream out
Her lover's turning off, turning on the television
And I can't tell the difference between
ABC News, Hill Street Blues and a preacher of
the old time gospel hour, stealing money from
the sick and the old.
For the God I believe in isn't short of cash, mister.
I feel a long way from the hills of San Salvador
Where the sky is ripped open and the rain pours
through a gaping wound
Pelting the women and children. . .
Who run. . .
Into the arms of America.

55

THE STAR SPANGLED BANNER

WORDS AND MUSIC BY
JIMI HENDRIX

SEGUE "BULLET THE BLUE SKY"

WHEN LOVE COMES TO TOWN

I was a sailor, I was lost at sea
I was under the waves before love rescued me
I was a fighter, I could turn on a thread
But I stand accused of the things I've said

When love comes to town
I want to jump that train
When love comes to town
I want to catch that flame
Maybe I was wrong to ever let you down
But I did what I did, before love came to town

I used to make love under a red sunset
I was making promises I was soon to forget
She was pale as the lace of her wedding gown
But I left her standing before love came to town

I ran into a juke joint when I heard a guitar scream
The notes were turning blue
When I fell into a dream
As the music played I saw my life turn around
That was the day before love came to town

When love comes to town
I want to jump that train
When love comes to town
I want to catch that flame
Maybe I was wrong to ever let you down
But I did what I did, before love came to town

When I woke up I was sleeping on the street
I felt the world was dancing
And I was dirt beneath their feet
When I looked up I saw the Devil looking down
My Lord He played guitar the day love came to town

I was there when they crucified my Lord
I held the scabbard when the soldier drew his sword
I threw the dice when they pierced his side
But I've seen love conquer the great divide

When love comes to town
I want to jump that train
When love comes totown
I want to catch that flame
Maybe I was wrong to ever let you down
But I did what I did, before love came to town

WHEN LOVE COMES TO TOWN

WORDS BY BONO

MUSIC BY U2

I was a sail - or, I was lost at sea, ___ I was

un - der the waves, ___ be - fore love ___ res - cued me. ___

I was a fight - er, I could turn on a thread, ___ but

I stand ac - cused ___ of the things I've said. ___ Love ___

CHORUS

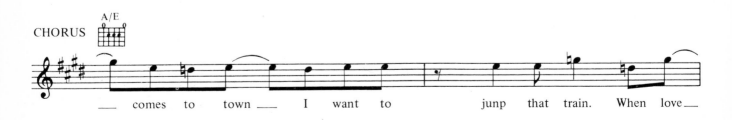

___ comes to town ___ I want to jump that train. When love ___

comes to town I want to catch that flame.

May - be I was wrong ___ to ev - er let you down, ___ but I

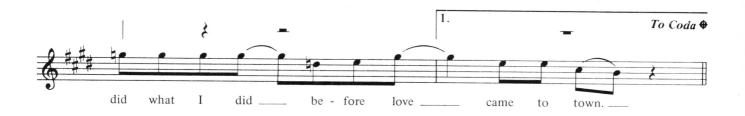

did what I did ___ be - fore love ___ came to town. ___

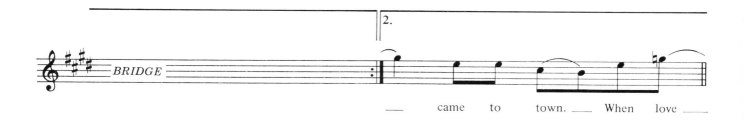

___ came to town. ___ When love ___

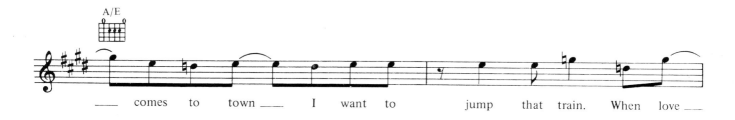

___ comes to town ___ I want to jump that train. When love ___

___ comes to town I want to catch that flame.

may - be I was wrong ___ to ev - er let you down, ___ but I

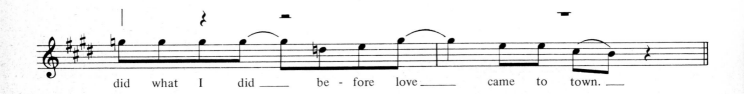

did what I did ___ be - fore love ___ came to town. ___

D.C. al Coda ⊕*CODA*

 INSTRUMENTAL SOLO

 INSTRUMENTAL TO FADE

VERSE 2:
I used to make love under a red sunset
I was making promises was soon to forget
She was pale as the lace of her wedding gown
But I left her standing before love came to town.

CHORUS 2:
I ran into a juke joint when I heard a guitar scream
The notes were turning blue
When I fell into a dream
As the music played I saw my life turn around
That was the day before love came to town.

CHORUS 1:
Love comes to town I want to jump that train.
When love comes to town I want to catch that flame.
Maybe I was wrong to ever let you down,
But I did what I did before love came to town.

VERSE 3:
I was there when they crucified my Lord
I held the scabbard when the soldier drew his sword
I threw the dice when they piereced his side
But I've seen love conquer the great divide.

REPEAT CHORUS 1:

ANGEL OF HARLEM

It was a cold and wet December day
When we touched down at JFK
Snow was melting on the ground
On BLS I heard the sound (of an Angel)

New York like a Christmas tree
I said tonight this city belongs to me (Angel)

Soul Love this love won't let me go
So long ... Angel of Harlem

Birdland on 53
The street sounds like a symphony
We got John Coltane and a love supreme
Miles and she has to be an Angel

Lady Day got diamond eyes
She sees the truth behind the lies (Angel)

Soul Love this love won't let me go
So long ... Angel of Harlem

Blue light on the avenue
God knows thye got to you
An empty glass, the lady sings
Eyes swollen like a bee sting
Blinded you lost your way
On the side streets and the alleyways
Like a star exploding in the night
Filling up the city with broad daylight
an Angel in Devil's shoes
Salvation in the blues
You never looked like an Angel
So long ... Angel of Harlem

ANGEL OF HARLEM

WORDS BY BONO

MUSIC BY U2

It was a cold and wet De-cem-ber day __ when we touched the ground __ at J. F. K. __
Bird-land __ on 53 __ the street sounds like __ a sym-pho-ny, we got

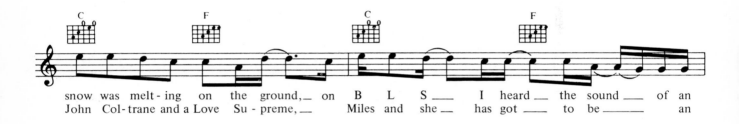

snow was melt-ing on the ground, __ on B L S __ I heard __ the sound __ of an
John Col-trane and a Love Su-preme, __ Miles and she __ has got __ to be __ an

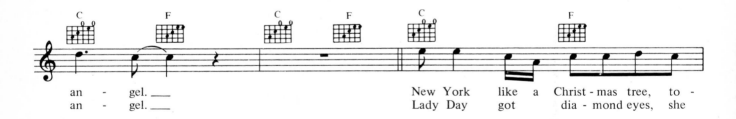

an - gel. __
an - gel. __   New York   like a Christ-mas tree, to -
                                          Lady Day   got   dia - mond eyes, she

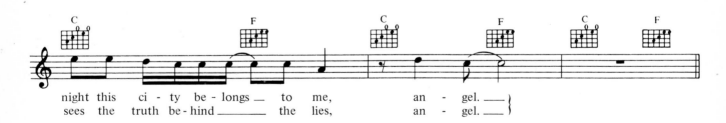

night this ci - ty be - longs __ to me,   an - gel. __ }
sees the truth be - hind __ the lies,   an - gel. __ }

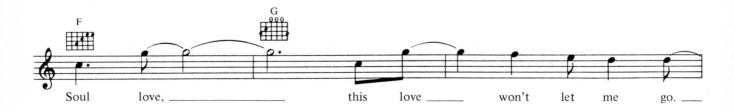

Soul   love, __   this love __ won't let me go. __

So long, _____ an - gel of

Har - lem. ____ 2° (An - gel of Har - lem. __)

Ooh _____ ooh _____ she says

heart _____ heart ___ and soul. _____

Blue light on the av - en - ue, God knows they got to you, an
Blind - ed, you lost your way, on the side streets and the al - ley ways, like a

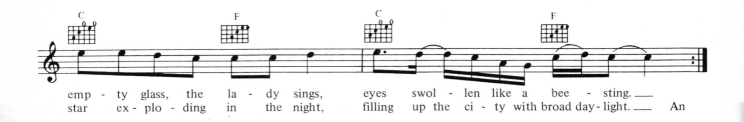

emp - ty glass, the la - dy sings, eyes swol - len like a bee - sting. ___
star ex - plo - ding in the night, filling up the ci - ty with broad day - light. ___ An

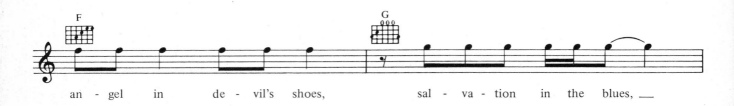

an - gel in de - vil's shoes, sal - va - tion in the blues, ___

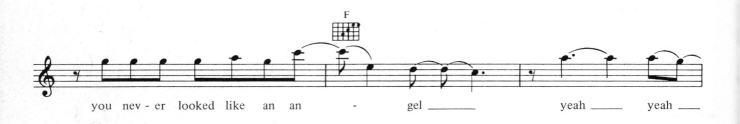

you nev - er looked like an an - gel ___ yeah ___ yeah ___

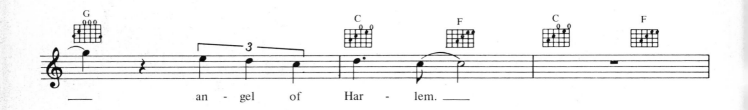

___ an - gel of Har - lem. ___

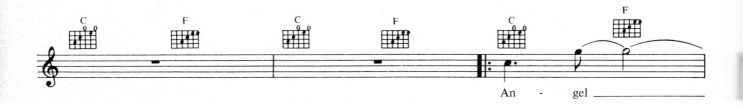

An - gel ___

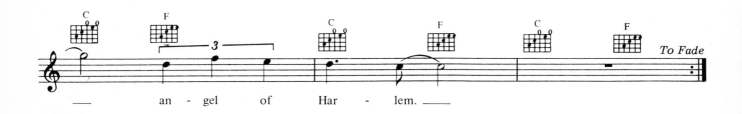

___ an - gel of Har - lem.

ALL ALONG THE WATCHTOWER

"There must be some way out of here,"
said the joker to the thief,
"There's too much confusion,
I can't get no relief.
Businessmen they drink my wine,
plowmen dig my earth,
None of them along the line
know what any of it is worth."

"No reason to get excited,"
the thief, he kindly spoke,
"There are many here among us
who feel that life is but a joke.
But you and I, we've been through that,
and this is not our fate,
So let us not talk falsely now,
the hour is getting late."

All along the watchtower,
princes kept the view
While all the women came and went,
barefoot servants, too.
Outside in the distance
a wildcat did growl,
Two riders were approaching,
the wind began to howl.

ALL ALONG THE WATCHTOWER

WORDS AND MUSIC BY
BOB DYLAN

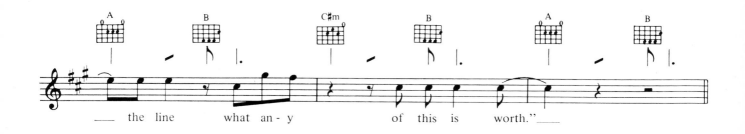

the line   what an-y   of this is   worth."

VERSE 2:
"No reason to get excited," the thief, he kindly spoke,
"There are many here among us who feel that life is but a joke.
But you and I, we've been through that, and this is not our fate,
So let us not talk falsely now, the hour is getting late."

VERSE 3:
All along the watchtower, princes kept the view
While all the women came and went, barefoot servants, too.
Outside in the distance a wildcat did growl,
Two riders were approaching, the wind began to howl.

VERSE 4:
All I got is a red guitar,
Three chords and the truth.
All I got is a red guitar,
The rest is up to you.

VERSE 5: (AS VERSE 2:)

I STILL HAVEN'T FOUND
WHAT I'M LOOKING FOR

I have climbed the highest mountains
I have run through the fields
Only to be with you
Only to be with you

I have run I have crawled
I have scaled these city walls
Only to be with you
But I still haven't found
What I'm looking for
But I still haven't found
What I'm looking for

I have kissed honey lips
Felt the healing in her fingertips
It burned like fire
This burning desire
I have spoke with the tongue of angels
I have held the hand of a devil
It was warm in the night

I was cold as a stone
But I still haven't found
What I'm looking for
But I still haven't found
What I'm looking for

I believe in the Kingdom Come
Then all the colours will bleed into one
But yes I'm still running
You broke the bonds
You loosed the chains
You carried the cross
And my shame
And my shame
You know I believe it
But I still haven't found
What I'm looking for
But I still haven't found
What I'm looking for

I STILL HAVEN'T FOUND WHAT I'M LOOKING FOR

WORDS BY BONO

MUSIC BY U2

I have climbed ___ the high-est moun-tains, I have run ___ through the

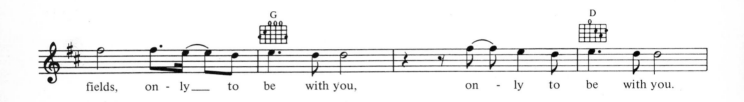

fields, on - ly ___ to be with you, on - ly to be with you.

1,3,5.

2,4,6.

2. I have
4. I have
6. You broke the

But I still _____ have- n't found

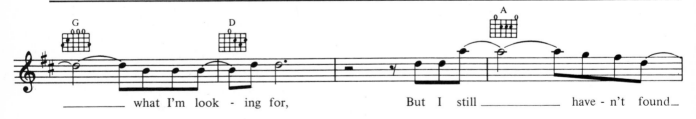

_____ what I'm look - ing for, But I still _____ have- n't found

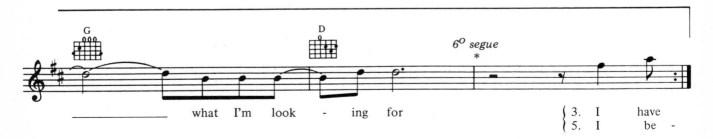

_____ what I'm look - ing for

6° *segue*
*

3. I have
5. I be -

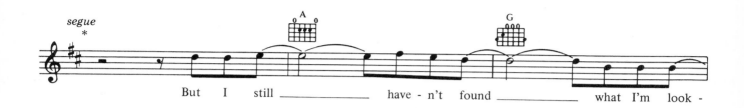

But I still _____ have-n't found _____ what I'm look -

- ing for, But I still _____ have-n't found _

_____ what I'm look - ing for.

Ad lib. to Fade

VERSE 2:
I have run I have crawled
I have scaled these city walls
These city walls
Only to be with you.

VERSE 3:
I have kissed honey lips
Felt the healing in her fingertips
It burned like fire
This burning desire.

VERSE 4:
I have spoke with the tongue of angels
I have held the hand of a devil
It was warm in the night
I was cold as a stone.

VERSE 5:
I believed in the Kingdom Come
Then all the colours will bleed into one
Bleed into one
But yes I'm still running.

VERSE 6:
You broke the bonds you loosed the chains
You carried the cross and my shame
And my shame
You know I believe it.

LOVE RESCUE ME

Love rescue me
Come forth and speak to me
Raise me up and don't let me fall
No man is my enemy
My own hands imprison me
Love rescue me

Many strangers have I met
On the road to my regret
Many lost who seek to find themselves in me
They ask me to reveal
The very thought they would conceal
Love rescue me

And the sun in the sky makes a shadow of you and I
Stretching out as the sun sinks in the sea
I'm here without a name in the palace of my shame
Love rescue me

In the cold mirror of a glass
I see my reflection pass
I see the dark shades of what I used to be
I see the purple of her eyes
The scarlet of my lies
Love rescue me

And the sun in the sky makes a shadow of you and I
Stretching out as the sun sinks in the sea
I'm hanging by my thumbs
I'm ready for whatever comes
Love rescue me

Yea though I walk through the valley of the shadow
Yet I will fear no evil
I have cursed thy rod and staff
They no longer comfort me
Love rescue me

Sha la la sha la la
Sha la la sha la la

I've conquered my past
The future is here at last
I stand at the entrance
To a new world I can see
The ruins to the right of me
Will soon have lost sight of me
Love rescue me

LOVE RESCUE ME

WORDS BY BONO & BOB DYLAN

MUSIC BY U2

Love res - cue me, come forth and ___ speak to me.

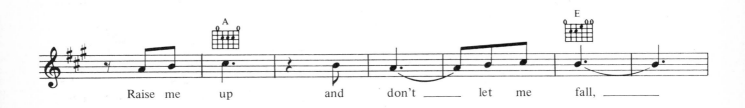

Raise me up and don't ___ let me fall, ___

no man is my ___ e - ne - my, my own hands im -

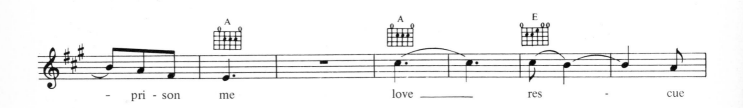

- pri - son me love ___ res - cue

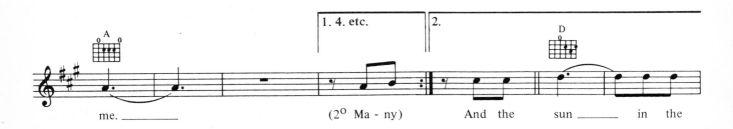

me. ___ (2° Ma - ny) And the sun ___ in the

sky ____ makes a sha-dow ____ of you and I, stretch-ing

out as the sun sinks ____ in the sea. ____

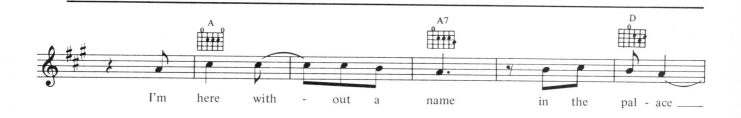

I'm here with - out a name in the pal - ace ____

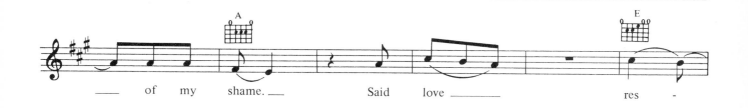

____ of my shame. ____ Said love ____ res -

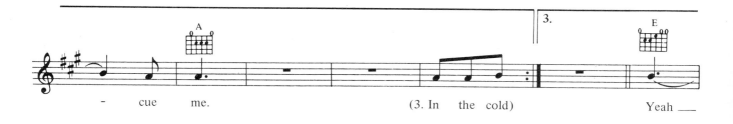

3.

- cue me. (3. In the cold) Yeah ____

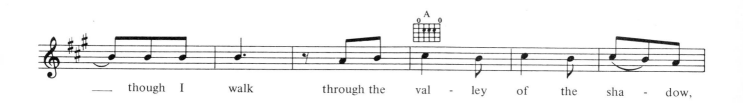

____ though I walk through the val - ley of the sha - dow,

Yet ____ I will fear ____ no ____

ev - il. I have cursed thy ____ rod and staff,

they no lon - ger ____ com - fort me. Love ____

Repeat ad lib. to Fade

____ res - cue me.

VERSE 2:
Many strangers have I met
On the road to my regret
Many lost who seek to find themselves in me
They ask me to reveal
The very thoughts they would conceal
Love rescue me.

VERSE 3:
In the cold mirror of a glass
I see my reflection pass
I see the dark shades of what I used to be
I see the purple of her eyes
The scarlet of my lies
Love rescue me.

VERSE 4:
Sha la la sha la la
Sha la la sha la la

VERSE 5:
I've conquered my past
The future is here at last
I stand at the entrance
To a new world I can see
The ruins to the right of me
Will soon have lost sight of me
Love rescue me.

Printed in England
Panda Press · Haverhill · Suffolk • 9/89

Book Designed by Steve Averill
Works Associates Ltd., Dublin
Photography by Anton Corbijn
Bill Rubenstein, Colm Henry,
David Aron and Tom Busier
Music Transcribed by Roger Day
(Except titles on pages 10, 54 and 78)
Music Processed by Musicprint Ltd.
Printed by Panda Press · Haverhill · Suffolk